Cat
TRIVIA

Published by Willow Creek Press, Inc.
P.O. Box 147, Minocqua, Wisconsin 54548

Printed in the United States

Cat
TRIVIA

OVER 200 AMEOWZING FELINE
FACTS FOR CAT LOVERS

■ WILLOW CREEK PRESS®

CATS CAN VOCALIZE UP TO
24 SOUNDS, EACH WITH
A SPECIFIC MEANING.

WITH 20 MILLION SCENT RECEPTORS WITHIN ITS
NOSE, A CAT'S ABILITY TO SMELL IS 40 TIMES
MORE POWERFUL THAN THAT OF MERE HUMANS.

EACH CAT'S NOSE PRINT IS DISTINCT AND
UNIQUE, JUST LIKE A HUMAN FINGERPRINT.

CATS ALSO HAVE WHISKERS ON THE
BACK OF THEIR FRONT LEGS.

ADULT CATS HAVE 30 TEETH;
KITTENS HAVE 26.

WITH LESS THAN 500 TASTE BUDS ON
THEIR TONGUE, COMPARED WITH 10,000
FOR HUMANS, IT CAN BE ARGUED THAT
CATS ARE ELEGANT BUT HAVE NO TASTE.

CATS ARE THOUGHT TO
BE IMITATING SNAKES
WHEN THEY HISS.

WHAT HAPPENS WHEN
CATS ARE CONFUSED?

THEY BECOME PURRPLEXED

CATS SPEND HALF THEIR WAKING HOURS GROOMING THEMSELVES WITH THEIR RASPY TONGUE. THEY ALSO SPEND SIGNIFICANT TIME HACKING UP FUR BALLS RESULTING FROM GROOMING.

CATS SHARE OVER 95% OF THEIR GENETIC MAKEUP WITH TIGERS.

FAMILY MEMBERS IN ANCIENT EGYPT TYPICALLY SHAVED THEIR EYEBROWS IN MOURNING FOR THE PASSING OF A PET CAT.

CATS HAVE A UNIQUE ORGAN LOCATED
BEHIND THEIR UPPER INCISORS ALLOWING
THEM TO TASTE SCENTS IN THE AIR.

IF A CAT QUICKLY SLAPS YOU WITH RETRACTED
CLAWS, IT'S PLAYING - NOT ANGRY.

CATS ARE COLOR BLIND TO A DEGREE
- THEY MOSTLY SEE THE WORLD IN
SHADES OF GRAY, YELLOW, AND BLUE.

WHAT GREATER GIFT THAN
THE LOVE OF A CAT.

-CHARLES DICKENS

A CAT WALKED INTO A BAR AND
ORDERED A SHOT OF WHISKEY.

HE SLOWLY NUDGED IT WITH
HIS PAW UNTIL IT WENT
CRASHING TO THE FLOOR.

THE CAT SAID TO THE
BARTENDER, "I'LL
HAVE ANOTHER."

TAYLOR SWIFT'S CAT "OLIVIA" HAS A
REPORTED NET WORTH OF $97 MILLION.
SHE'S BELIEVED TO BE THE THIRD-
RICHEST PET IN THE WORLD.

SIAMESE CATS ARE THOUGHT
TO HAVE ORIGINATED IN
THAILAND DURING THE 14TH
CENTURY. THIS MAKES THEM
ONE OF THE OLDEST CAT
BREEDS IN THE WORLD.

WHAT DO CATS EAT ON HOT DAYS?

MICE CREAM

WHAT'S A CAT'S FAVORITE COLOR?

PURRPLE

IN 1963, FELICETTE BECAME THE FIRST
(AND ONLY) CAT TO EXPERIENCE
AND SURVIVE SPACEFLIGHT.

BECAUSE A FEMALE CAT'S OVARIES RELEASE
NUMEROUS EGGS DURING HER DAYS
IN HEAT, THE KITTENS IN HER LITTER
CAN HAVE MORE THAN ONE FATHER.

CAT BREEDERS ARE
CALLED "CATTERIES."

THERE ARE FEW THINGS IN LIFE
MORE HEARTWARMING THAN TO
BE WELCOMED BY A CAT.

-TAY HOHOFF

"CHIEF MOUSER" IS THE OFFICIAL TITLE OF THE CURRENT CAT RESIDING AT 10 DOWNING STREET. THE DESIGNATION DATES BACK TO THE YEAR 1515.

ABRAHAM LINCOLN LOVED CATS.
HE FED "TABBY" WITH A GOLD FORK
AT WHITE HOUSE DINNERS.

CATS UTILIZE THEIR TAILS FOR BALANCE
WHEN WALKING UPON NARROW LEDGES.

BLACKIE THE CAT INHERITED THE
EQUIVALENT OF $12.5 MILLION WHEN
HIS OWNER, BEN REA, DIED IN 1988.

IN A CAT'S EYE, ALL THINGS
BELONG TO CATS.

-ANONYMOUS

GRUMPY CAT WAS ONCE AN INTERNET SENSATION WITH MORE THAN 2.6 MILLION INSTAGRAM FOLLOWERS AND 1.5 MILLION TWITTER FOLLOWERS. GRUMPY'S REAL NAME WAS "TARTAR SAUCE."

PRESIDENT CALVIN COOLIDGE
SUCCESSFULLY USED A SPECIAL
RADIO BROADCAST APPEALING
TO THE PUBLIC TO FIND HIS
CAT THAT WENT MISSING
FROM THE WHITE HOUSE.

WHERE DOES A CAT GO AFTER LOSING ITS TAIL?

THE RE-TAIL STORE

WHAT'S A CAT'S FAVORITE BUTTON ON A TV REMOTE?

PAWS

CATS CURL THEIR LIPS INTO WHAT LOOKS LIKE A SNEER. THIS ODD FACIAL EXPRESSION RESULTS WHEN THEY ORALLY TRAP SCENT PHEROMONES FROM OTHER CATS.

A COP STOPS A MAN IN A CAR WITH A MOUNTAIN LION IN THE FRONT SEAT.

THE COP SAID, "YOU SHOULD TAKE THAT TO THE ZOO."

"THAT'S A GOOD IDEA!" THE MAN SAID.

THE NEXT WEEK THE SAME COP STOPS THE SAME MAN WITH THE SAME MOUNTAIN LION SITTING BESIDE HIM.

"I THOUGHT YOU WERE GOING TO TAKE THAT TO THE ZOO," SAID THE COP.

"I DID," THE MAN REPLIED. "WE HAD SUCH A GOOD TIME THAT WE'RE GOING TO THE BEACH THIS WEEKEND!"

THE SELKIRK REX IS THE NEWEST
RECOGNIZED CAT BREED.
IT'S ALSO CALLED THE "POODLE CAT"
DUE TO ITS CURLY, THICK FUR.

A MAINE COON CAT NAMED "STEWIE"
MEASURED 48.5 INCHES LONG.
HE WAS THE LONGEST DOMESTIC
CAT EVER MEASURED.

WHAT'S A CAT'S FAVORITE MAGAZINE?

GOOD MOUSEKEEPING

WHISKERS PREDICTABLY SIGNAL A CAT'S MOOD. WHISKERS PINNED BACK INDICATE FEAR; WHISKERS FORWARD SIGNIFY CURIOSITY.

THE RITUAL OF CATS GROOMING OTHER CATS IS CALLED "ALLOGROOMING."

SOME CATS CAN SWIM.

WHY WAS THE CAT SITTING
ON THE COMPUTER?

TO KEEP AN EYE ON THE MOUSE

WHAT DO YOU GET WHEN YOU CROSS
A SNOWMAN WITH A TIGER?

FROSTBITE

PERHAPS ONE REASON WE ARE
FASCINATED BY CATS IS BECAUSE
SUCH A SMALL ANIMAL CAN CONTAIN
SO MUCH INDEPENDENCE, DIGNITY
AND FREEDOM OF SPIRIT. UNLIKE
THE DOG, THE CAT'S PERSONALITY IS
NEVER BET ON HUMANS. HE DEMANDS
ACCEPTANCE ON HIS OWN TERMS.

-LLOYD ALEXANDER

IT IS ADVISED THAT A SINGLE-CAT HOUSEHOLD HAVE TWO LITTER BOXES. TWO CATS SHOULD SHARE THREE LITTER BOXES.

THE PROBLEM WITH CATS IS THAT THEY
GET THE SAME LOOK WHETHER THEY
SEE A MOTH OR AN AXE MURDERER.

-PAULA POUNDSTONE

CATS HAVE IT ALL:
ADMIRATION, AN ENDLESS
SLEEP, AND COMPANY ONLY
WHEN THEY WANT IT.

-ROD MCKUEN

ONLY 86% OF CATS ARE
SPAYED OR NEUTERED.
THAT'S WHY ROUGHLY 700
MILLION FERAL CATS ROAM
THE UNITED STATES.
CONVERSELY, IT IS ESTIMATED
THAT THE U.S. HAS 88
MILLION PET CATS.

EDGAR ALLAN POE'S CAT "CATARINA" INSPIRED HIS STORY, "THE BLACK CAT."

CATS HAVE A THIRD EYELID THAT SERVES AS A SHIELD FOR THE CORNEA.

A CAT'S LEARNING ABILITY IS EQUIVALENT TO THAT OF A THREE-YEAR-OLD.

A LIE IS LIKE A CAT: YOU
NEED TO STOP IT BEFORE IT
GETS OUT THE DOOR OR IT'S
REALLY HARD TO CATCH.

-CHARLES M. BLOW

CATS BUMP THEIR
HEADS ON PEOPLE AS
A SIGN OF AFFECTION.

"JENNY" WAS THE OFFICIAL CAT OF THE TITANIC. THE FELINE MASCOT HELPED CONTROL THE SHIP'S RODENT POPULATION.

ANCIENT EGYPTIANS REVERED BLACK
CATS DUE TO THEIR RESEMBLANCE
TO THE GODDESS "BASTET."

THERE ARE FOUR TABBY CAT PATTERNS:
CLASSIC, SPOTTED, TICKED, AND MACKEREL.

CATS CAN ATTAIN A RUNNING SPEED OF
30 MPH OVER SHORT DISTANCES.

CATS MAY FART WHEN
FRIGHTENED.

CATS LIE ON THEIR OWNER'S
CHESTS FOR WARMTH,
COMFORT, AND SECURITY.
THEY KNOW THAT NO ONE'S
GOING ANYWHERE WITHOUT
THEM BEING AWARE OF IT.

IN 2004 ARCHEOLOGISTS IN
CYPRUS DISCOVERED THE
GRAVE OF A CAT DATING
BACK 9,500 YEARS.

WHAT DO YOU CALL A CAT
WHO LOVES TO BOWL?

AN ALLEY CAT

WHY ARE CATS BETTER THAN BABIES?

YOU ONLY HAVE TO CHANGE THE
LITTER BOX ONCE A DAY

CATS' COLLARBONES ARE BURIED
IN THEIR SHOULDER MUSCLES AND
CONNECT TO NO OTHER BONES.

WHEN RUBBING ITS BODY AND FACE AGAINST
YOU, A CAT CLAIMS OWNERSHIP OF YOU.

STUBBS, THE CAT, WAS MAYOR OF TALKEETNA,
ALASKA, UNTIL HIS DEATH IN 2017.

CATS HAVE TINY GLANDS IN
THEIR PAWS THAT EMIT A
STRONG SCENT DETECTED
BY OTHER CATS, SERVING AS
A FORM OF RECOGNITION.

LIKE CAMELS AND GIRAFFES,
CATS SIMULTANEOUSLY MOVE
THEIR PAWS FROM EACH SIDE
OF THEIR BODY WHEN WALKING.
THIS TRAIT IS UNIQUE TO
THESE THREE SPECIES.

PICKY CATS CAN STUBBORNLY
REFUSE HEALTHY BUT
DISDAINED FOODS TO THE
EDGE OF STARVATION.

IT IS IMPOSSIBLE TO KEEP A
STRAIGHT FACE IN THE PRESENCE
OF ONE OR MORE KITTENS.

-CYNTHIA E. VARNADO

WHAT HAPPENS WHEN CATS
GO ON A FIRST DATE?

THEY HISS

WHY ARE KITTENS EXCELLENT BOSSES?

THEY DISPLAY GREAT LITTERSHIP

IT IS PURPORTED THAT CAT
"MEOWING" IS A UNIQUE
BEHAVIOR DEVELOPED TO
COMMUNICATE WITH HUMANS.

A KITTEN IS THE DELIGHT OF
A HOUSEHOLD. ALL DAY LONG
A COMEDY IS PLAYED OUT BY
AN INCOMPARABLE ACTOR.

-CHAMPFLEURY

CATS DRINKING FROM THE TAP
IS AN ANCESTRAL TRAIT.
IT'S SAFER TO DRINK FROM RUNNING
WATER THAN A STAGNANT POND OR POOL.

A FEMALE CAT CAN BECOME PREGNANT
AS YOUNG AS FOUR MONTHS OLD.

CATS WERE FIRST BROUGHT TO COLONIAL
AMERICA TO RID THE TERRITORY OF RODENTS.

A GROUP OF KITTENS IS
CALLED A "KINDLE."

CALICO CATS ARE SAID TO BRING
GOOD LUCK TO THEIR HOMES.

CATS CHATTER THEIR TEETH.
IT'S A SIGN OF EXCITEMENT
OR FRUSTRATION.

OWNERS ARE ADVISED TO ROTATE
THEIR CAT'S TOYS TO KEEP THINGS
NEW AND INTERESTING.

IN 2007, "WINNIE" THE CAT
AWAKENED AN INDIANA
FAMILY AFTER DETECTING
DANGEROUS LEVELS OF CARBON
MONOXIDE IN THEIR HOME.
THE FAMILY SURVIVED
THE INCIDENT.

"UNSINKABLE SAM" WAS THE NICKNAME FOR A CAT THAT SURVIVED THE SINKING OF THE GERMAN BATTLESHIP BISMARCK AND TWO OTHER BRITISH WARSHIPS.
HE REMAINS THE MOST FAMOUS MASCOT OF THE ROYAL NAVY.

CATS DOING THEIR "DUTY" OUTSIDE THEIR LITTER BOX IS THE MOST COMMON COMPLAINT AMONG OWNERS. THE REASONS FOR THIS ARE NUMEROUS, BUT HOUSEHOLD CHANGES (VISITORS OR THE PRESENCE OF A NEW PET, FOR EXAMPLE) ARE THE PRIMARY CAUSES.

POLYDACTYL CATS, LIKE THE FAMOUS CATS
THAT HAVE LIVED AT ERNEST HEMINGWAY'S
KEY WEST HOME FOR GENERATIONS, HAVE
EXTRA TOES ON THEIR FRONT PAWS.

HOW IS CAT FOOD SOLD?

PURR THE CAN

IF LIGHTS RUN ON ELECTRICITY AND
CARS ON GAS, WHAT DO CATS RUN ON?

THEIR PAWS

NO HOME IS COMPLETE WITHOUT THE PITTER-PATTER OF KITTY FEET.

-ANONYMOUS

WHEN A CAT LIES ON ITS BACK, EXPOSING ITS BELLY, IT IS A SIGN OF TRUST - NOT NECESSARILY AN INVITE TO A BELLY RUB.

A CAT'S FLEXIBLE SPINE CONTAINS 53 VERTEBRAE. HUMANS, BY CONTRAST, HAVE ONLY 34.

CATS FIND IT THREATENING WHEN YOU STARE DIRECTLY AT THEM.

IN 1997, "KETZEL," THE TUXEDO CAT, WON AN AWARD FOR HIS PIANO COMPOSITION.

CATS CHASE LASERS BECAUSE IT PROVOKES THEIR STRIKE INSTINCT.

EXPERTS CAN SAFELY ASSUME
CATS DREAM WHILE ASLEEP
BECAUSE THEY EXHIBIT REM
(RAPID EYE MOVEMENT).

HOW DO CATS END A FIGHT?

THEY HISS AND MAKE UP

WHAT DO CATS SAY BEFORE
CHASING MICE?

"LET US PREY"

CATS EERILY STARE INTO SPACE. THE OPTICS CAN BE WEIRD, BUT MOST LIKELY, THEY ARE CONCENTRATING ON ULTRASONIC FREQUENCIES WE CAN'T HEAR.

THE CLAWS EMBEDDED IN A CAT'S PAWS CURVE DOWNWARD. WHILE THIS IS HANDY FOR CLIMBING UP TREES, THEY CAN ONLY CLIMB DOWN BY DESCENDING BACKWARD.

SOME CATS HABITUALLY
CHEW ON FABRICS,
METALS, OR PLASTIC.
THIS IS A RARE CONDITION
CALLED "PICA," TREATED BY
ADDITIONAL SMALL DAILY
MEALS AND CHEW TOYS.

WHISKERS HELP A CAT DECIDE WHETHER
IT CAN ENTER A SMALL SPACE.

CATS WILL OFTEN STEAL AND HIDE OBJECTS
SUCH AS FEATHER DUSTERS, SMALL
STUFFED TOYS, AND OTHER OBJECTS THAT
REMIND THEM OF PREY ANIMALS.

THE LONGEST RECORDED JUMP BY
A DOMESTIC CAT WAS SIX FEET.

CATS RAISE THEIR BUTTS AS
A GESTURE OF GREETING.

WHEN ROME BURNED, THE
EMPEROR'S CATS STILL
EXPECTED TO BE FED ON TIME.

-SEANAN MCGUIRE

CATS KNOW HOW TO OBTAIN FOOD WITHOUT
LABOR, SHELTER WITHOUT CONFINEMENT,
AND LOVE WITHOUT PENALTIES.

-W.L. GEORGE

PEOPLE WITH CAT ALLERGIES
AREN'T SENSITIVE TO FUR;
RATHER, THEY ARE REACTING
TO A PROTEIN FOUND IN CAT
URINE, SALIVA, AND DANDER.

CATS PAW AT AND KNOCK
OVER SMALL OBJECTS IN
HOPES OF STARTLING HIDING
MICE AND OTHER RODENTS.

CATS LOVE TO LIE ON WHATEVER
ITEM YOU'RE USING AT THE
TIME, INCLUDING LAPTOPS.
IT'S THEIR WAY OF LAYING
CLAIM TO NOT ONLY YOU
BUT YOUR STUFF AS WELL.

STANDING CATS FAVORABLY
REACT TO PETTING BY ABRUPTLY
LIFTING THEIR BUTTS.

THIS SIGNAL OF FELINE
PLEASURE IS CALLED THE
"ELEVATOR BUTT."

I HAVE BEEN TOLD THAT THE TRAINING
PROCEDURE WITH CATS IS VERY DIFFICULT.
IT'S NOT. MINE TRAINED ME IN TWO DAYS.

-BILL DANA

WHY DON'T CATS PLAY POKER IN THE JUNGLE?

TOO MANY CHEETAHS

WHY WAS THE CAT SO SMALL?

IT ONLY DRANK CONDENSED MILK

CATS CAN EASILY HEAR THE
ULTRASONIC SOUNDS CREATED BY
MICE AND OTHER RODENTS.
ALSO, WITH 32 MUSCLES ALLOWING THE
180-DEGREE ROTATION OF EACH EAR
INDEPENDENTLY, THEY CAN PINPOINT
THE LOCATION OF THEIR PREY.

A CAT CURLING ITS TAIL IN THE SHAPE OF A
QUESTION MARK IS ASKING YOU TO PLAY.

CATS HAVE TWICE AS MANY NEURONS IN
THEIR CEREBRAL CORTEX AS DOGS.

PURRING HELPS CATS DEAL WITH STRESS
AND ILLNESS AND HELPS WITH HEALING.

A HAPPY ARRANGEMENT:
MANY PEOPLE PREFER CATS TO
OTHER PEOPLE, AND MANY CATS
PREFER PEOPLE TO OTHER CATS.

-MASON COOLEY

CATS HAVE KEEN NIGHT AND
PERIPHERAL VISION AND CAN
DETECT MOVEMENTS AND IMAGES
80% BETTER THAN HUMANS IN
LOW-LIGHT CONDITIONS.

CATS HAVE A TOTAL OF 230 BONES.
HUMANS HAVE 206 BONES.

CATS THAT LIVE INDOORS HAVE
LIFE SPANS RANGING FROM 12 TO
20 YEARS, WHILE OUTDOOR CATS
TYPICALLY LIVE 3 TO 10 YEARS.

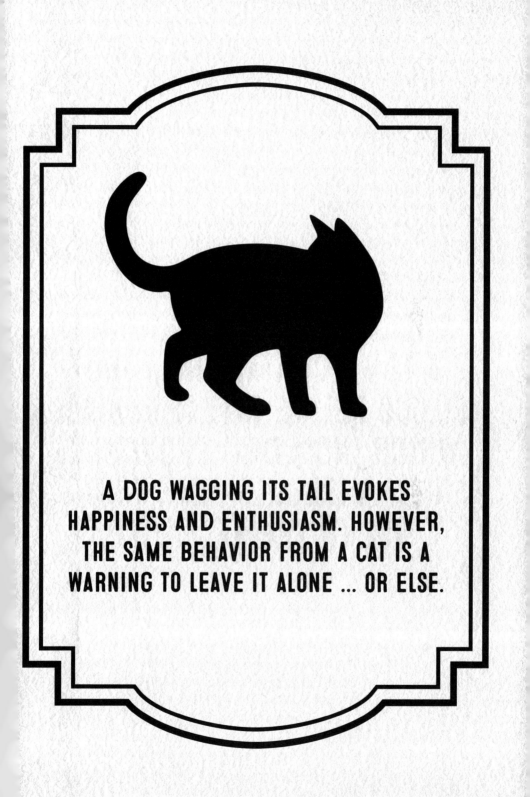

A DOG WAGGING ITS TAIL EVOKES HAPPINESS AND ENTHUSIASM. HOWEVER, THE SAME BEHAVIOR FROM A CAT IS A WARNING TO LEAVE IT ALONE ... OR ELSE.

IN 1888, ARCHEOLOGISTS IN
MIDDLE EGYPT DISCOVERED
A TOMB CONTAINING ABOUT
80,000 FELINE RITUAL BURIALS,
WHICH INCLUDED PROVISIONS
OF MICE AND MILK FOR
USE IN THE AFTERLIFE.

WHAT IS A CAT'S FAVORITE TV SHOW?

CLAW AND ORDER

WHAT DO CATS LOOK FOR IN A FRIEND?

A GREAT PURRSONALITY

OWNERS OF DOGS WILL HAVE NOTICED THAT IF
YOU PROVIDE THEM WITH FOOD AND WATER
AND SHELTER AND AFFECTION, THEY WILL
THINK YOU ARE GOD. WHEREAS OWNERS OF
CATS ARE COMPELLED TO REALIZE THAT, IF
YOU PROVIDE THEM WITH FOOD AND WATER
AND SHELTER AND AFFECTION, THEY DRAW
THE CONCLUSION THAT THEY ARE GOD.

-CHRISTOPHER HITCHENS

EAR TWITCHING IN CATS REFLECTS A
SENSE OF ANXIETY OR IRRITATION.

CATS LIKE TO EAT GRASS, FOLLOWING
THEIR WILD ANCESTORS' LEAD.

CATS JUMP OVER FIVE TIMES THEIR HEIGHT.

99% OF CALICO CATS
ARE FEMALE.

CATS ALSO USE THEIR TAILS AS
TOKENS OF TRUST AND FRIENDSHIP
WHEN DRAPING THEM OVER YOU
OR OTHER HUMANS AND ANIMALS.

AS ANYONE WHO HAS
EVER BEEN AROUND A CAT
FOR ANY LENGTH OF TIME
WELL KNOWS, CATS HAVE
ENORMOUS PATIENCE WITH THE
LIMITATIONS OF MANKIND.

-CLEVELAND AMORY

"CREAM PUFF" WAS THE NAME OF THE OLDEST KNOWN CAT TO EVER LIVE. SHE LIVED IN AUSTIN, TEXAS, FROM AUGUST 3, 1967 TO AUGUST 2005.

CATS ARE MOST OFTEN ACTIVE
DURING DAWN AND DUSK.

A CAT APPROACHING YOU WITH A STRAIGHT,
"SHIVERING" TAIL IS DELIGHTED TO SEE YOU.

DOGS HAVE BEEN DOMESTICATED FOR 5,000
YEARS LONGER THAN CATS WHICH MAY HELP
EXPLAIN THE FELINE INDEPENDENCE STREAK.

ROUGHLY 200 FERAL CATS ARE ALLOWED
TO OCCUPY DISNEYLAND FOR THE
PURPOSE OF RODENT CONTROL.

A CAT HAS ABSOLUTE EMOTIONAL
HONESTY: HUMAN BEINGS, FOR
ONE REASON OR ANOTHER,
MAY HIDE THEIR FEELINGS,
BUT A CAT DOES NOT.

-ERNEST HEMINGWAY

A CAT'S JAW CAN'T MOVE SIDEWAYS.

CATS DEVELOP SPECIFIC VOCALIZATIONS
WITH THEIR OWNER THAT THEY
SHARE WITH NO ONE ELSE.

IN ADDITION TO ACUTE NIGHT VISION, CATS
SEE DISTANT OBJECTS VERY WELL. HOWEVER,
NEARBY ITEMS TEND TO BE BLURRY.

WHAT DO CATS USE TO MAKE COFFEE?

A PURRCOLATOR

HOW DO CATS BUY THINGS?

THROUGH A CATALOG, OF COURSE

LIKE THEIR ANCESTORS, CATS INSTINCTIVELY CIRCLE BEFORE THEY LIE DOWN TO MAKE SURE THEY ARE DOWNWIND FROM THE APPROACH OF PREY OR PREDATORS.

WHISKERS ARE DEEPLY EMBEDDED
AND CONTAIN HIGHLY SENSITIVE
NERVE ENDINGS THAT HELP CATS
NAVIGATE - ESPECIALLY IN THE DARK.

CATS CAN GO A BIT CRAZY LATE AT NIGHT WHEN THEIR OWNERS ARE IN BED. THEY SOMETIMES RACE THROUGHOUT THE HOUSE, JUMPING ON AND OFF FURNITURE IN A GENERALLY HARMLESS BEHAVIOR CALLED "CAT ZOOMIES."

KITTENS "KNEAD" THEIR MOTHERS WITH THEIR PAWS TO STIMULATE MILK FLOW. ADULT CATS CONTINUE THE PRACTICE, PERHAPS SENTIMENTALLY, TO ENCOURAGE CONTENTMENT.

ONE FEMALE CAT CAN PRODUCE
ABOUT 49,000 KITTENS.

CATS LEAVE PREY AT YOUR DOORSTEP
AS AN ACT OF KINDNESS.

LILIES AND DAFFODILS ARE HARMFUL
TO CATS WHO CHEW ON THEM.

CATS' BRAINS CONTAIN SHORT- AS
WELL AS LONG-TERM MEMORY.

A GREEN CAT WAS BORN IN DENMARK IN 1995. OFFICIALS BELIEVE THAT HIGH LEVELS OF COPPER IN THE NEIGHBORHOOD WATER PIPES WERE RESPONSIBLE.

WHAT HAPPENED TO THE CAT THAT ATE A LEMON?

HE BECAME A SOURPUSS

WHAT DID THE INTUITIVE CAT SAY?

"I JUST HAD A STRONG FELINE"

A MAN WALKS INTO A BAR
WITH A CAT AND A DOG.

THEY ALL SIT DOWN AS THE BARTENDER
ASKS, "WHAT CAN I GET YOU?"

THE DOG REPLIES, "I'LL HAVE A
GIN AND TONIC, THE GUY WILL
HAVE A BEER, AND THE CAT
WANTS A VODKA MARTINI."

THE STUNNED BARTENDER
TELLS THE DOG, "MY GOSH,
YOU'RE A TALKING DOG!"

THE MAN LOOKS AT THE BARTENDER
AND SAYS, "DON'T BE FOOLED;
THE CAT IS A VENTRILOQUIST."

CARTOONIST JIM DAVIS HAILS
FROM FAIRMONT, INDIANA
WHERE THE GARFIELD TRAIL
HONORS HIS BELOVED FELINE
CHARACTER WITH MORE
THAN A DOZEN STATUES.

RITUAL SCRATCHING SHARPENS CLAWS
WHILE STRETCHING THOSE MUSCLES IN
THE TORSO THAT CANNOT BE EXERCISED
DURING REGULAR STRETCHING.

AFTER A CONFRONTATION, A CAT MAY YAWN
TO END THE SITUATION PEACEFULLY.

USE POSITIVE REINFORCEMENT;
CATS ARE HIGHLY TRAINABLE.

CATS NORMALLY SPEND 70% OF
THEIR LIVES SLEEPING.

A GROUP OF CATS IS CALLED A "CLUTTER,"
"CLOWDER," OR "GLARING."

TABBY CATS HAVE A DISTINCTIVE "M"
MARK ON THEIR FOREHEAD FUR.

I BELIEVE CATS TO BE SPIRITS
COME TO EARTH. A CAT, I AM
SURE, COULD WALK ON A CLOUD
WITHOUT COMING THROUGH.

-JULES VERNE

A CONTENTED CAT GIVING YOU A SLOW-
BLINK IS THROWING YOU A "KITTY KISS."
ON THE OTHER HAND, STARING AT A CAT IS
PERCEIVED AS AN ACT OF AGGRESSION.

CATS LOVE TO SHELTER AND LURK IN TIGHT SPACES SUCH AS CARDBOARD BOXES IN RESPONSE TO PRIMITIVE URGES TO HIDE FROM PREDATORS AS WELL AS OBSERVING PREY.

WHAT IS A CAT'S FAVORITE SPORT?

HAIRBALL

LICKING ALSO SOOTHES PAINFUL OR
IRRITATED AREAS ON A CAT'S BODY.

MOST FEMALE CATS ARE RIGHT-PAWED,
WHILE MALES ARE LIKELY LEFT-PAWED.
SOME ARE AMBIDEXTROUS.

THE PRESENCE OF A LITTER BOX SPARKS
A PRIMAL INSTINCT IN CATS WHOSE
ANCESTORS HID THEIR WASTE TO ELIMINATE
THEIR SCENT FROM PREDATORS. CATS
ALSO BURY THEIR FOOD FOR THE SAME
REASON THEY BURY THEIR WASTE.

THE ACT OF LICKING RELEASES ENDORPHINS THAT MAKE CATS CONTENT. IT ALSO STIMULATES BLOOD FLOW TO THE SKIN.

UP TO 50% OF CATS LACK THE GENE THAT REACTS TO CATNIP.

CATS HAVE ROUGHLY 100 VARIOUS VOCALIZATIONS, WHILE DOGS HAVE ONLY TEN.

A CAT'S TAIL CONTAINS 23 BONES.

PRESIDENT ABRAHAM LINCOLN LOVED CATS AND KEPT UP TO FOUR OF THEM IN THE WHITE HOUSE AT ANY GIVEN TIME. "NO MATTER HOW MUCH CATS FIGHT," LINCOLN FAMOUSLY OBSERVED, "THERE ALWAYS SEEMS TO BE PLENTY OF KITTENS."

CAT FACIAL WHISKERS ARE ROUGHLY
EQUAL IN LENGTH TO THE WIDTH OF
THEIR BODY. THEY ARE UTILIZED TO FEEL
AND SENSE THEIR ENVIRONMENT.

HEBREW LEGEND ATTESTS THAT
GOD CREATED CATS AFTER NOAH
PRAYED FOR HELP PROTECTING
GRAIN STORAGE ABOARD
THE ARK FROM RODENTS. HE
INDUCED A LION TO SNEEZE,
RESULTING IN THE SUDDEN
PRESENCE OF TWO CATS.

CATNIP CREATES A DISARMING RESPONSE IN CATS SIMILAR TO MARIJUANA IN HUMANS. IT IS CAUSED BY THE CHEMICAL NEPETALACTONE AND WEARS OFF WITHIN 15 MINUTES OR SO.

HISSING IS AN EXPRESSION OF FEAR
AND VULNERABILITY, NOT ANGER.

A CAT'S ROUGH TONGUE IS HANDY
FOR LICKING MEAT OFF A BONE.

AN ADULT CAT BRAIN IS
APPROXIMATELY TWO INCHES LONG.

KITTENS ARE ANGELS WITH WHISKERS.

-ALEXIS FLORA HOPE